WE READ ABOUT

LIVING WITH AUTISM

WRITTEN BY CHRISTINA EARLEY
AND MADISON PARKER

ILLUSTRATED BY
AMANDA HUDSON

Parent and Caregiver Guide

Reading aloud with your child has many benefits. It expands vocabulary, sparks discussion, and promotes an emotional bond. Research shows that children who have books read aloud to them have improved language skills, leading to greater school success.

I Read! You Read! books offer a fun and easy way to read with your child. Follow these guidelines.

Before Reading

- Look at the front and back covers. Discuss personal experiences that relate to the topic.
- Read the *Words to Know* at the back of the book. Talk about what the words mean.
- If the book will be challenging or unfamiliar to your child, read it aloud by yourself the first time. Then, invite your child to participate in a second reading.

During Reading

Have your child read the words beside this symbol. This text has been carefully matched to the reading and grade levels shown on the cover.

You read the words beside this symbol.

- Stop often to discuss what you are reading and to make sure your child understands.
- If your child struggles with decoding a word, help them sound it out. If it is still a challenge, say the word for your child and have them repeat it after you.
- To find the meaning of a word, look for clues in the surrounding words and pictures.

After Reading

- Praise your child's efforts. Notice how they have grown as a reader.
- Use the *Comprehension Questions* at the back of the book.
- Discuss what your child learned and what they liked or didn't like about the book.

Most importantly, let your child know that reading is fun and worthwhile. Keep reading together as your child's skills and confidence grow.

TABLE OF CONTENTS

I LIVE WITH AUTISM

Hi! My name is Summer.

I am nine years old.

I live with my mom, dad, older brother, and younger sister. Cookie is my bearded dragon.

I was born with autism and am **neurodivergent**.

I do not like to be hugged.

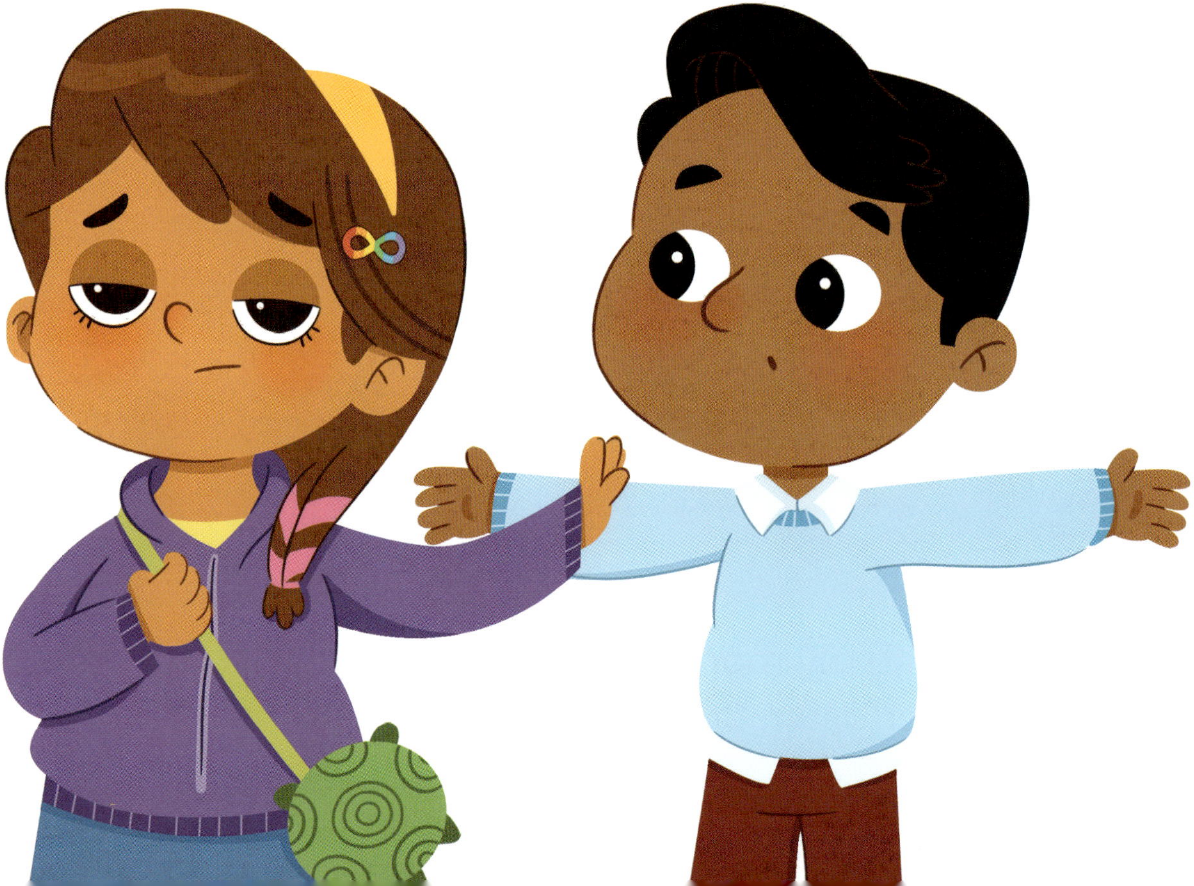

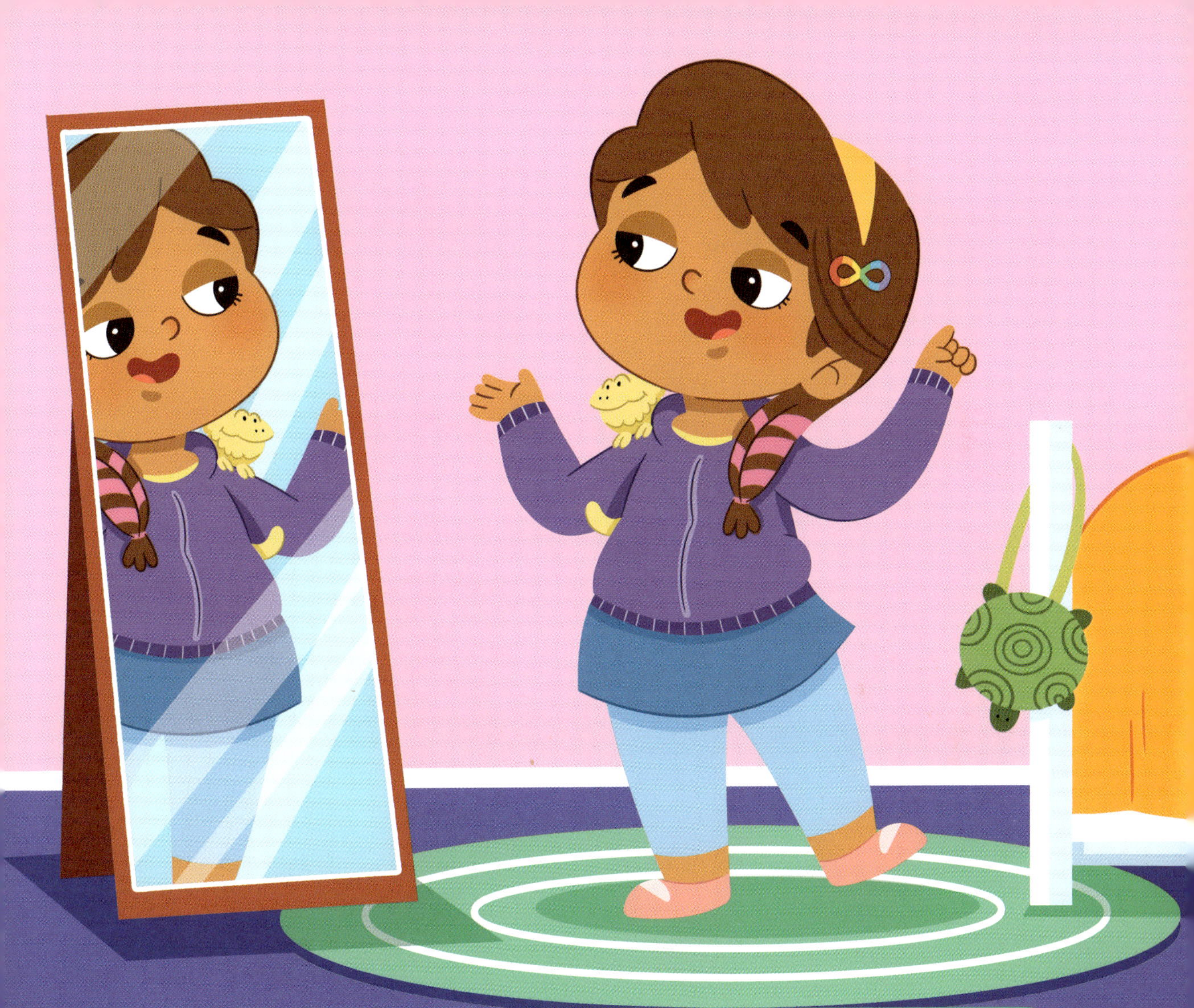

I get **anxious** when I **interact** with others.
I practice what I am going to say.

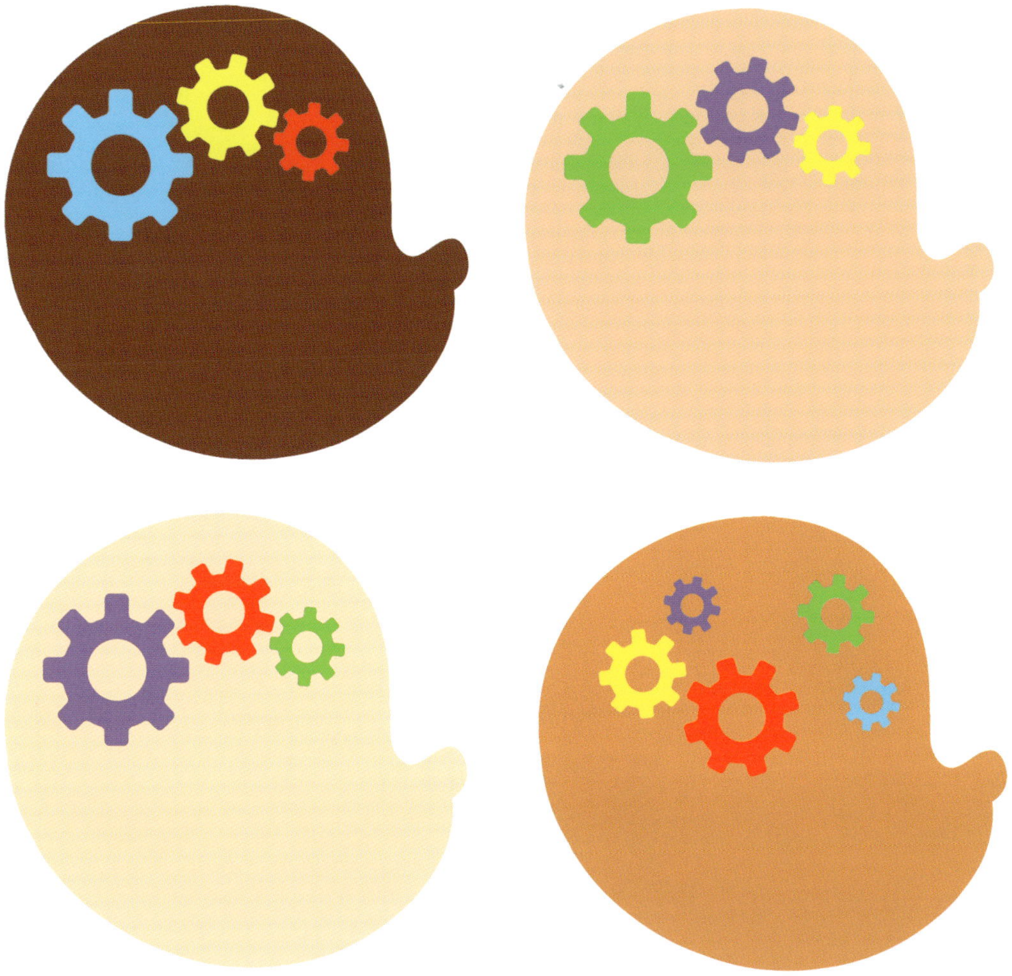

Autism is a **development** and brain **disorder**.

It affects how people communicate, learn, and behave.

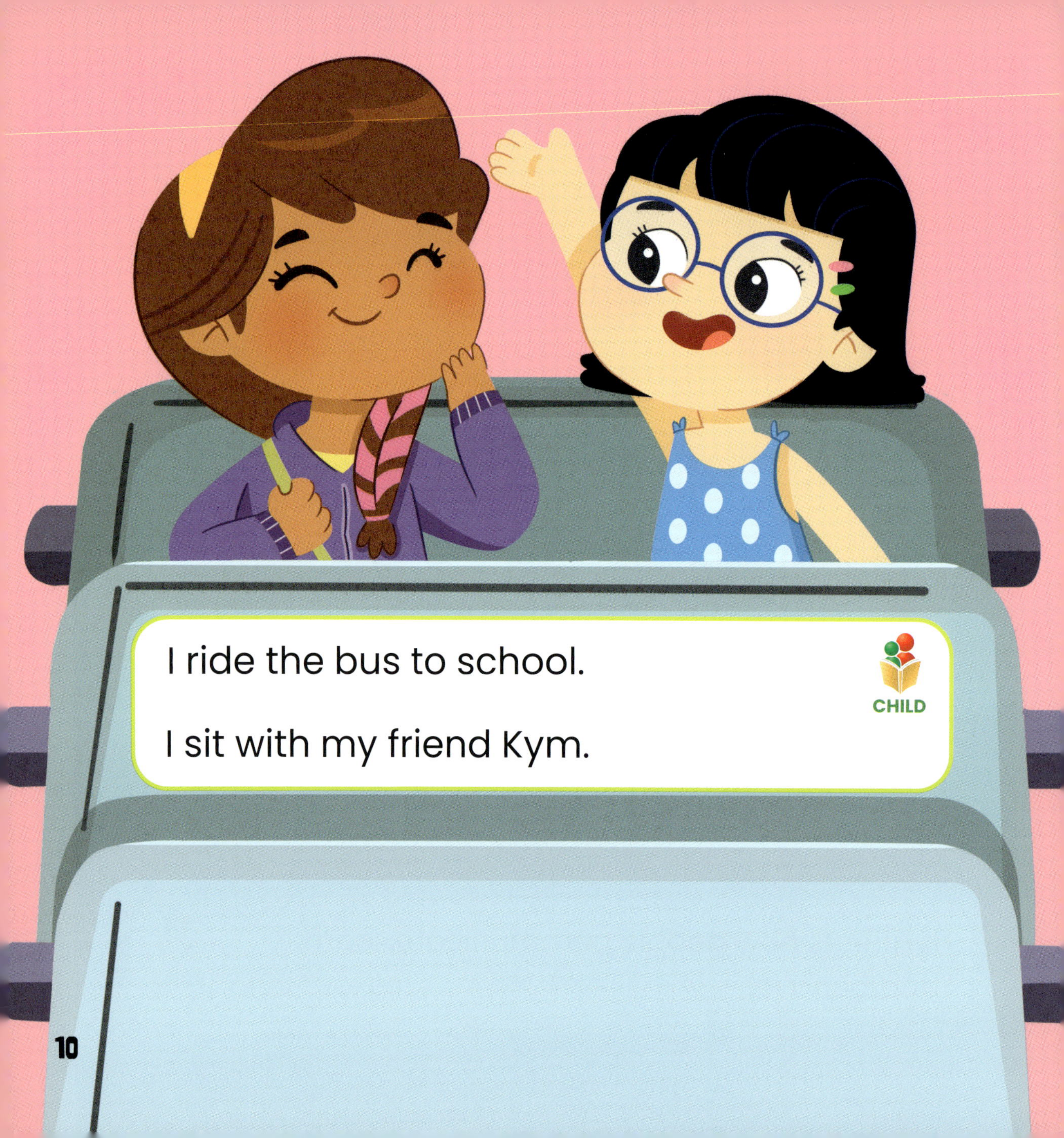

I ride the bus to school.

I sit with my friend Kym.

I tell Kym all about reptiles. I am an expert!

⏲	MON	TUE	WED	THU	FRI
9am					
10am					
12pm					
1pm					
2pm					

I have a schedule with pictures on my desk. I like to know what is coming next.

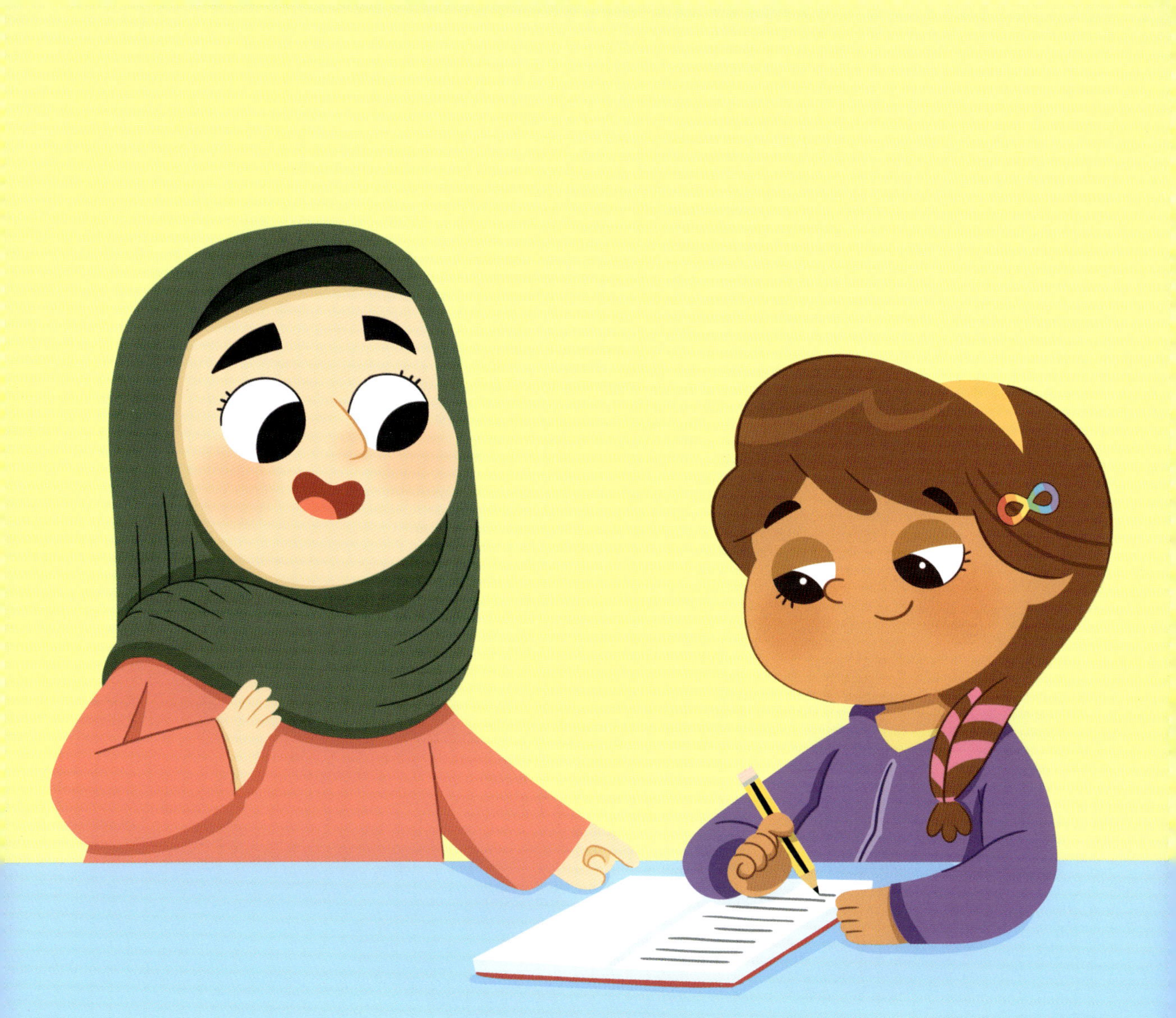

Miss April helps me with my classwork. She explains things to me again.

I always eat crunchy carrots and crispy pretzels for lunch.

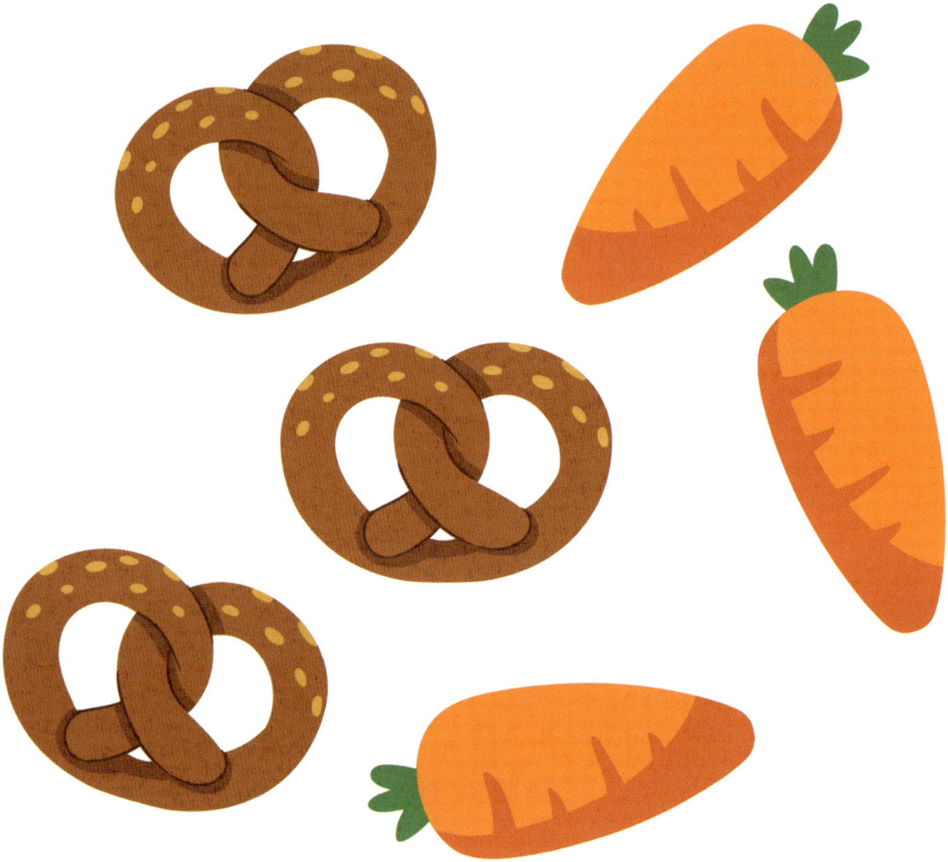

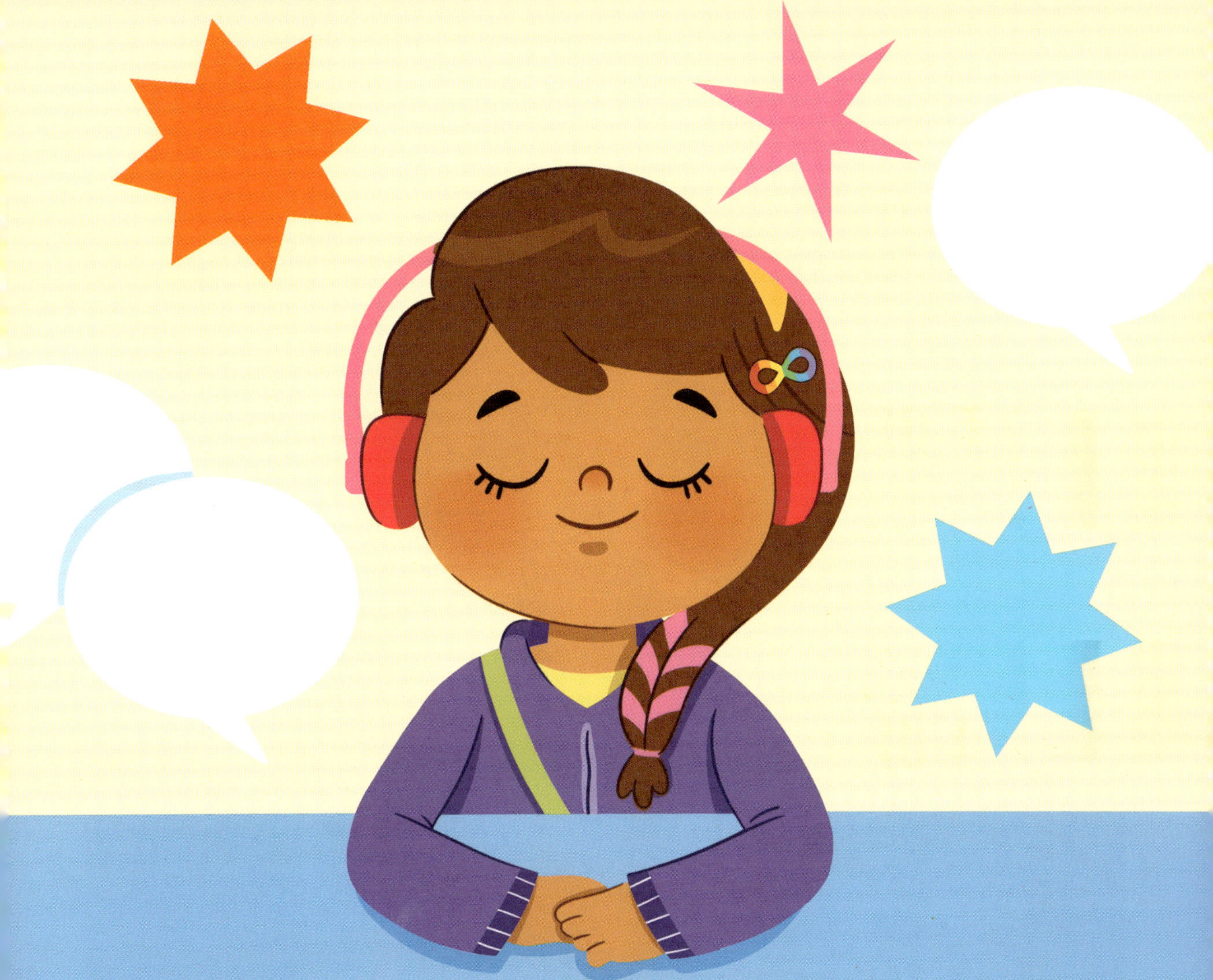

I wear headphones because the cafeteria is very loud.

My art teacher Mrs. Sakura sometimes lets me draw cartoons.

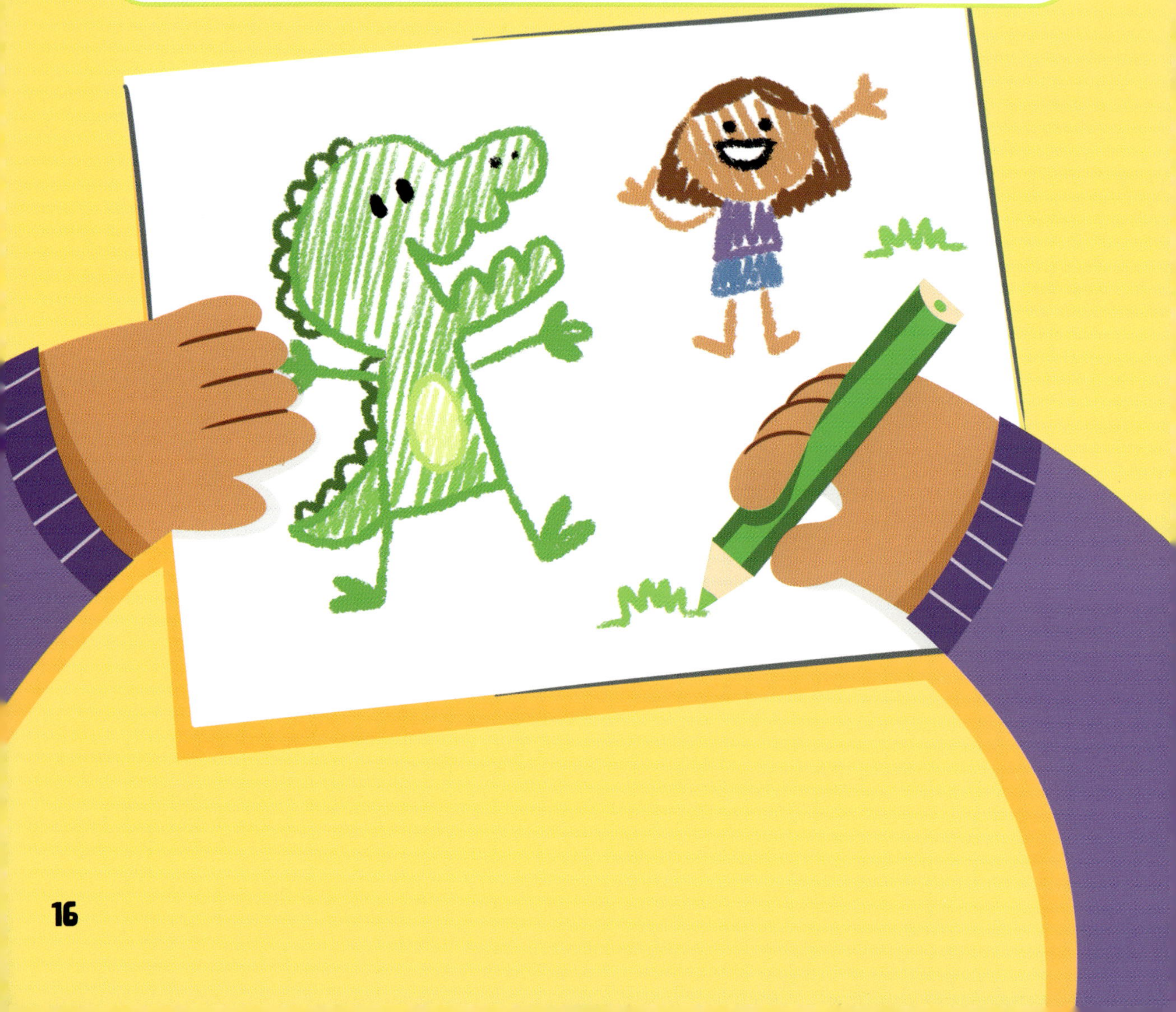

I would like to be an **animator** when I grow up. What would you like to be?

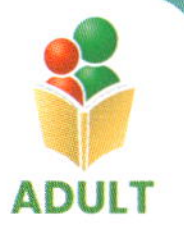

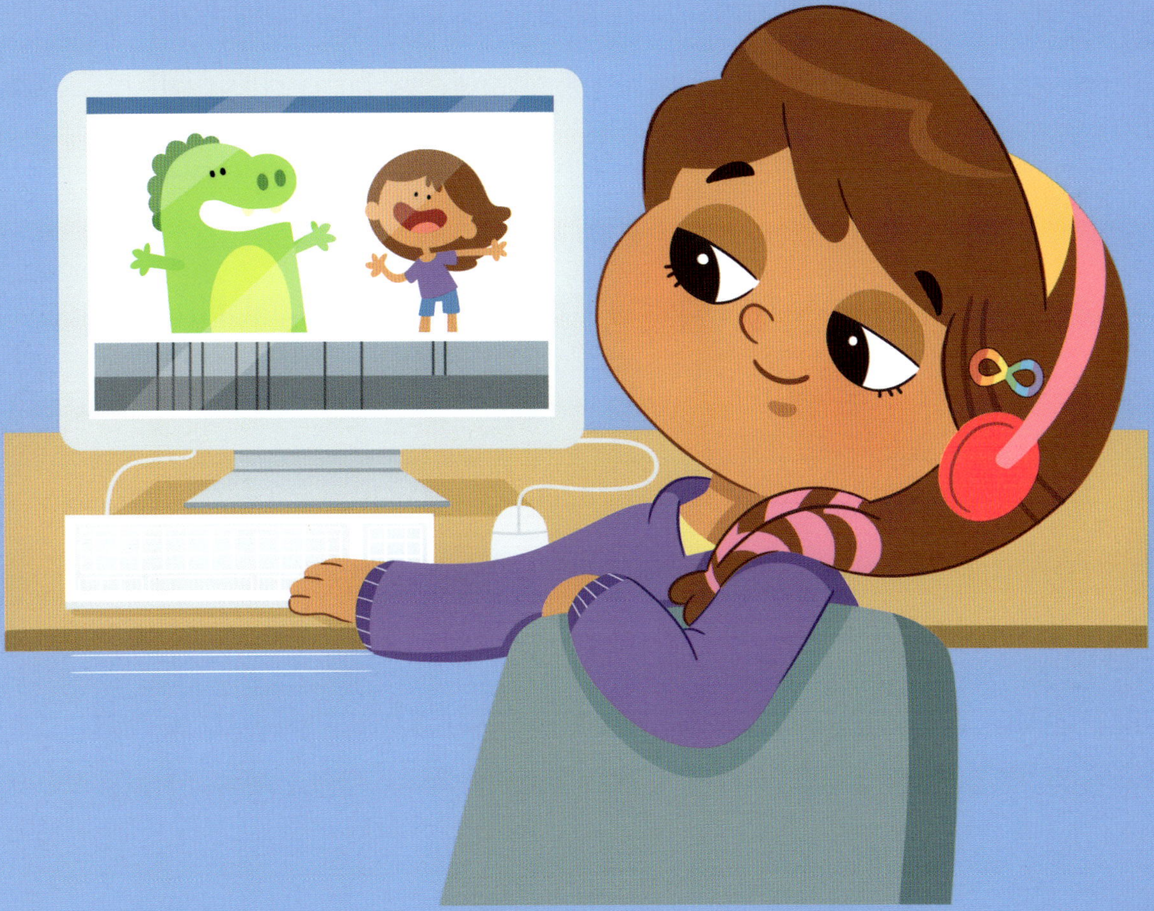

LEARN ABOUT AUTISM

What Is Autism?

Autism is a brain disorder that causes people to have restricted interests, repetitive behaviors, and difficulty with social communication and interaction. Not all people with autism will have all these. Autistic people use the word *neurodiverse* to explain the differences, abilities, and strengths of their brains.

Difficulty with social communication and interaction is common. Some autistic people do not seem to look at or listen to others who are talking. Others might talk about a particular topic, but not realize the other person is not interested. People with autism might have rigid routines.

Some are sensitive to temperature, texture, smell, or sound. Having strong specific interests is common.

People with autism also have strengths. Many excel in technical and logical subjects like science, engineering, and math. Being precise and detail-oriented is beneficial. Having a unique perspective allows for creative problem-solving.

Although autism is a lifelong condition, children and adults who are provided with the right supports can lead fulfilling lives in school, at work, in relationships, and in their communities.

Websites to Visit

Autism Highway: autismhwy.com

Autism Science Foundation: autismsciencefoundation.org

Autistic Inclusive Meets: autisticinclusivemeets.org

Autistic Self Advocacy Network: autisticadvocacy.org

Organization for Autism Research: researchautism.org

Take the Pledge for Inclusion

- ☑ I accept people of all abilities.
- ☑ I respect others and act with kindness and compassion.
- ☑ I include people with special needs and disabilities in my school and in my community.

Get your parent's permission to sign the online pledge at PledgeforInclusion.org.

Famous People with Autism

Lewis Carroll: Author of *Alice's Adventures in Wonderland*

Albert Einstein: Scientist and mathematician

Temple Grandin: Scientist

Lionel Messi: Professional soccer player

Satoshi Tajiri: Creator of Pokémon

Greta Thunberg: Environmental activist

Lionel Messi

Greta Thunberg

Celebrate and Educate

Neurodiversity Celebration Month happens in April.

World Autism Month happens in April.

World Autism Awareness Day is April 2nd.

Inclusive Schools Week is the first full week in December.

WORDS TO KNOW

animator (an-uh-MAY-tur): a person who draws cartoons that move

anxious (ANGK-shuhs): feeling nervous, worried, or fearful

development (di-VEL-uhp-muhnt): process of growing

disorder (dis-OR-dur): a physical or mental condition that is unusual

interact (in-tur-AKT): to respond to others and talk to them in a social situation

neurodivergent (nur-oh-dye-VER-juhnt): having a brain that works differently

INDEX

COMPREHENSION QUESTIONS

1. Summer has a pet ___.

a. snake

b. fish

c. bearded dragon

2. For lunch, Summer always eats foods that are ___.

a. soft

b. crunchy

c. cold

3. Autism is a disorder of the ___.

a. muscles

b. brain

c. skeleton

4. True or False: Summer likes to be hugged.

5. True or False: Summer likes to draw cartoons.

Answers: 1. c, 2. b, 3. b, 4. False, 5. True

Written by: Christina Earley and Madison Parker
Illustrated by: Amanda Hudson
Design by: Under the Oaks Media
Editor: Kim Thompson

Library of Congress PCN Data
We Read About Living with Autism / Christina Earley and Madison Parker
I Read! You Read!
ISBN 979-8-8873-5632-7 (hard cover)
ISBN 979-8-8873-5633-4 (paperback)
ISBN 979-8-8873-5634-1 (EPUB)
ISBN 979-8-8873-5635-8 (eBook)
Library of Congress Control Number: 2023932889

Printed in the United States of America.

Photos: A.Taoualit/Shutterstock: p. 21 (Lionel Messi); Antonello Marangi/Shutterstock: p. 21 (Greta Thunberg)

Seahorse Publishing Company
www.seahorsepub.com

Published in the United States
Seahorse Publishing
PO Box 771325
Coral Springs, FL 33077